# REMARKABLE PEOPLE

# Queen Elizabeth II

**Leslie Buffam**

e Explore other books at:
WWW.ENGAGEBOOKS.COM

VANCOUVER, B.C.

**e**➔ WWW.ENGAGEBOOKS.COM

*Queen Elizabeth II:* Level 2
Remarkable People
Leslie Buffam 1949 –
Text © 2024 Engage Books
Design © 2024 Engage Books

Edited by: A.R. Roumanis, Melody Sun,
Ashley Lee & Sarah Harvey
Design by: Mandy Christiansen

Text set in Arial Regular.
Chapter headings set in Fibra One Alt.

FIRST EDITION / FIRST PRINTING

LIBRARY AND ARCHIVES CANADA CATALOGUING IN PUBLICATION

Title: Queen Elizabeth II: Remarkable People / Leslie Buffam
Names: Buffam, Leslie, 1949- author

Identifiers:
ISBN 978-1-77878-671-6 (hardcover)
ISBN 978-1-77878-672-3 (softcover)
ISBN 978-1-77878-674-7 (pdf)
ISBN 978-1-77878-673-0 (epub)

Subjects:
LCSH: Biographies—Juvenile literature

Classification: SF426.5 .L44 20200 | DDC J636.7—DC23

This project has been made possible in part
by the Government of Canada.

Canada

# Contents

# Who Was Queen Elizabeth II?

Queen Elizabeth II was The Queen of the United Kingdom before King Charles II became King. She was also Queen of the **Commonwealth of Nations**. She became Queen on February 6, 1952.

**KEY WORD**

**Commonwealth of Nations:** a group of more than 50 countries.

1926 - 2022

Queen Elizabeth was Queen for 70 years. She died on September 8, 2022, at the age of 96. She **reigned** longer than anyone in British history.

**KEY WORD**

**Reigned:** ruled.

## Early Life

Princess Elizabeth was born in London, England, on April 21, 1926. She was the oldest daughter of The Duke and Duchess of York. Her parents would later become King George VI and Queen Elizabeth. She had one younger sister named Margaret.

Much of Princess Elizabeth's childhood was spent at the Royal Lodge in Windsor Park. Her family was very close. Her father described them as "us four." Princess Elizabeth's family called her Lilibet.

Princess Elizabeth loved horses and often went riding with her father.

## Education

Princess Elizabeth did not attend school. She was taught at home by a **governess** and visiting teachers.

**Governess:** a woman hired to teach children in their home.

8

Princess Elizabeth began to study history and law when her father became King. She did this so she would be prepared to one day become Queen.

KING GEORGE VI 1895-1952

## Great Britain During The Queen's Childhood

In the 1920s, Britain was trying to heal after World War I. Many people had lost loved ones during the war. Almost two million British soldiers had become **disabled**.

More than 880,000 British soldiers died during World War I.

**KEY WORD**

**Disabled:** when a person's mind or body makes it hard for them to do certain activities.

The time between 1929 and 1939 is known as the Great Depression. Many people were very poor and did not have homes or food. They could not find jobs.

## From Lilibet to Princess

King Edward VIII was Princess Elizabeth's uncle. He decided to stop being King in December of 1936. Princess Elizabeth's father became King George VI early in 1937.

King Edward VIII was King for less than a year.

Princess Elizabeth became next in line to the throne at age 10. That meant she would become Queen when her father died.

## Britain at War

Germany invaded Poland in 1939. Great Britain went to war to help Poland. The war did not end until 1945.

Between 35 million and 60 million people died during World War II.

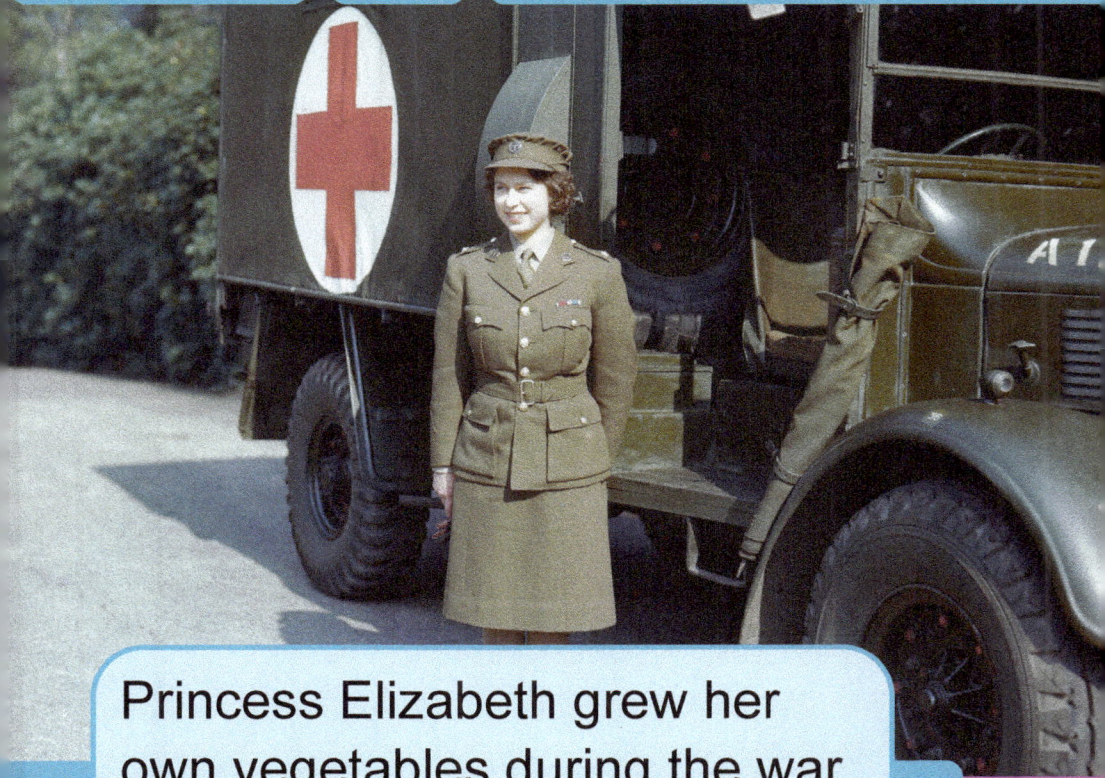

Princess Elizabeth grew her own vegetables during the war.

Princess Elizabeth stayed at Windsor Castle during the war. When Princess Elizabeth turned 18, she joined the British **Armed Forces**.

**KEY WORD**

**Armed Forces:** a country's military or army.

15

## Influences and Interests

The Queen's mother and grandmother were both great influences to her. They taught her how to handle life as a Royal.

Princess Elizabeth began riding horses at age three. As an adult, she raised and raced horses. She also loved dogs.

Corgis were The Queen's favorite dog. She owned more than 30 corgis in her lifetime.

## Personal Life

Princess Elizabeth first met her husband, Prince Philip of Greece, when she was eight. They wrote letters to each other during World War II. They got married in November 1947.

Princess Elizabeth and Prince Philip had four children. They are named Prince Charles, Princess Anne, Prince Andrew, and Prince Edward.

## Becoming Queen

Princess Elizabeth learned of her father's death while visiting Africa. She became Queen on February 6, 1952.

When Elizabeth became Queen, she promised her **subjects**, "Throughout all my life and with all my heart I shall strive to be worthy of your trust."

**KEY WORD**

**Subjects:** people who are ruled by a King or Queen.

## The Queen's Duties

The Queen worked with 15 different British **Prime Ministers** during her years on the throne. She met with them every week to talk about what was going on in the country.

**KEY WORD**

**Prime Ministers:** the leaders of governments that are chosen by the people in a country.

Prime Ministers carry important documents in a red case. It is called "the red box."

Queen Elizabeth II was a **symbol** of Britain. She went to many events and invited visitors from around the world to visit Britain. She also traveled to other countries.

**KEY WORD**

**Symbol:** something that represents or stands for something else.

# IT'S TRUE!
## Facts About Queen Elizabeth II

The Queen called her grandfather, King George V, "Grandpa England."

The Queen learned how to drive and fix trucks during World War II.

The Queen and Prince Philip's wedding cake was nine feet tall!

Every year, The Queen gave Christmas puddings to the people who worked for her.

The Queen's first corgi was named Susan.

The Queen wore colorful clothes and matching hats so she would be easy to see in public.

# TIMELINE

**April 21, 1926**
Queen Elizabeth II
is born

**November 29, 1934**
meets Prince Philip

**January 1, 1945**
joins the
Armed Forces

**May 1945**
end of World War II

**February 6, 1952**
King George VI dies.
Princess Elizabeth
becomes Queen
Elizabeth II.

**November 1953**
Queen Elizabeth II and
Prince Philip leave on
their first world tour

**March 10, 1964**
Prince Edward
is born

**September 2015**
becomes Britain's
longest reigning monarch

**December 1936**
becomes next in line
to be Queen

**September 1939**
start of World
War II

**November 20, 1947**
marries Prince Philip

**November 14, 1948**
Prince Charles
is born

**August 15, 1950**
Princess Anne is born

**February 19, 1960**
Prince Andrew
is born

**April 9, 2021**
Prince Philip dies

**September 8, 2022**
Queen Elizabeth II dies

# Be Like Queen Elizabeth II

If you would like to be like Queen Elizabeth II
- Do not be afraid of hard work.
- Give to others when you can.
- Spend time with family.

- Support other people's hard work.
- Be open to change.

# Quiz

Test your knowledge of Queen Elizabeth II by answering the following questions. The questions are based on what you have read in this book. The answers are listed on the bottom of the next page.

**1** What did Princess Elizabeth's family call her?

**2** Did Princess Elizabeth attend school?

**3** How many corgis did The Queen own in her lifetime?

**4** Where was Princess Elizabeth when she learned of her father's death?

**5** How many different British Prime Ministers did The Queen work with?

**6** What did The Queen learn during World War II?

# Explore other Readers.

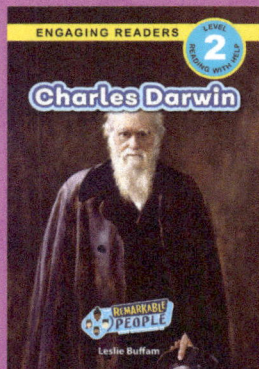

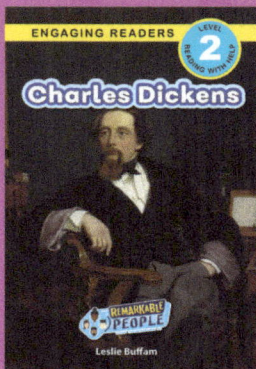

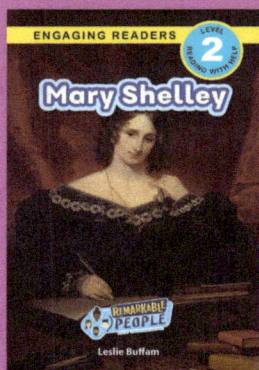

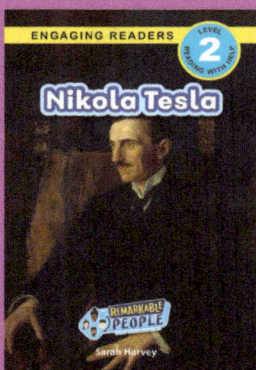

**ENGAGING READERS** · LEVEL 2 READING WITH HELP
**Charles Darwin**
REMARKABLE PEOPLE
Leslie Buffam

**ENGAGING READERS** · LEVEL 2 READING WITH HELP
**Charles Dickens**
REMARKABLE PEOPLE
Leslie Buffam

**ENGAGING READERS** · LEVEL 2 READING WITH HELP
**King Charles III**
REMARKABLE PEOPLE
Leslie Buffam

**ENGAGING READERS** · LEVEL 2 READING WITH HELP
**Mary Shelley**
REMARKABLE PEOPLE
Leslie Buffam

**ENGAGING READERS** · LEVEL 2 READING WITH HELP
**Nikola Tesla**
REMARKABLE PEOPLE
Sarah Harvey

**ENGAGING READERS** · LEVEL 2 READING WITH HELP
**Queen Elizabeth II**
REMARKABLE PEOPLE
Leslie Buffam

**ENGAGING READERS** · LEVEL 2 READING WITH HELP
**Gratitude**
EMOTIONS and FEELINGS
Kan Jones

**ENGAGING READERS** · LEVEL 2 READING WITH HELP
**Grief**
EMOTIONS and FEELINGS
Sarah Harvey

**ENGAGING READERS** · LEVEL 2 READING WITH HELP
**Love**
EMOTIONS and FEELINGS
Sarah Harvey

Visit www.engagebooks.com/readers

**Answers:** 1. Lilibet 2. No 3. More than 30 4. Africa 5. Fifteen 6. How to drive and fix trucks

www.ingramcontent.com/pod-product-compliance
Lightning Source LLC
Chambersburg PA
CBHW051239020426
42331CB00016B/3449